This Book Belongs to

_____

CHILDREN'S CHOICE®

For my father and little Marc,
from Maureen

Compilation copyright © 1981 by Jill Bennett
Illustrations copyright © 1981 by Maureen Roffey
Originally published in Great Britain 1981
by The Bodley Head Ltd.

Printed in U.S.A.
ISBN 0-590-75931-0

Days Are
Where We Live

and other poems

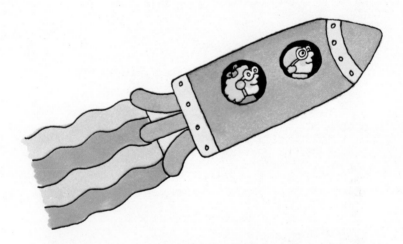

compiled by **JILL BENNETT**

illustrated by **MAUREEN ROFFEY**

 A Children's Choice® Book Club Edition From Scholastic Book Services

from
DAYS

What are days for?
Days are where we live.
They come, they wake us
Time and time over.
They are to be happy in:
Where can we live but days?

Philip Larkin

WAKING

My secret way of waking
is like a place
to hide.
I'm very still,
my eyes are shut.
They all think I am sleeping
but
I'm wide awake inside.

They all think I am sleeping
but

I'm wiggling my toes.
I feel sun-fingers
on my cheek.
I hear voices whisper-speak.
I squeeze my eyes
to keep them shut
so they will think I'm sleeping
BUT
I'm really wide awake inside
–and no one knows!

Lilian Moore

NEW CLOTHES AND OLD

I rather like New Clothes,
They make me feel so fine,
Yet I am not quite Me,
The clothes are not quite mine.

I really love Old Clothes,
They make me feel so free,
I know that they are mine,
For I feel just like Me.

Eleanor Farjeon

NEW SHOES

My shoes are new and squeaky shoes,
They're very shiny, creaky shoes,
I wish I had my leaky shoes
That mother threw away.

I liked my old brown leaky shoes
Much better than these creaky shoes,
These shiny, creaky, squeaky shoes
I've got to wear today.

Anon.

HAIR

There's
Curly hair
Straight hair
Fine hair
Strong.
Black hair
Blonde hair
Short hair
Long.
Who cares
If my hair's
Every sort of wrong?
Hair!

Wash it

Dry it

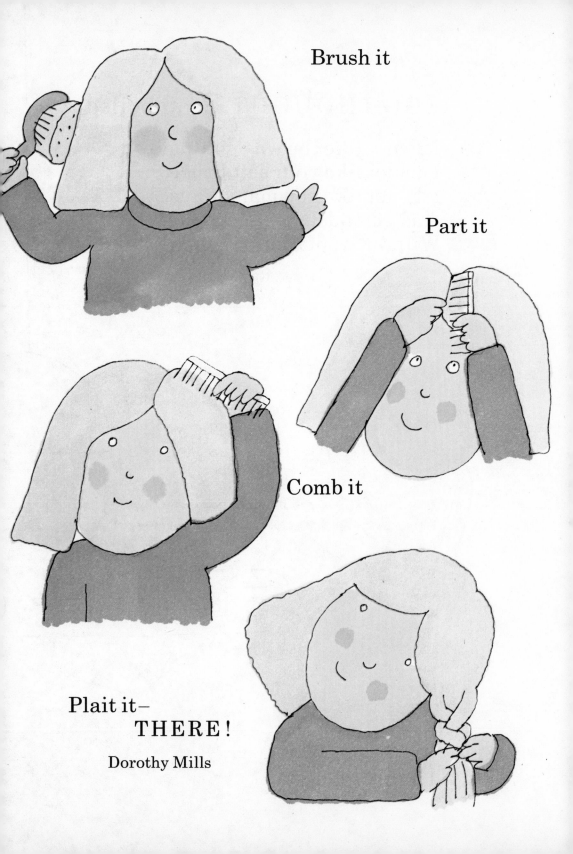

Brush it

Part it

Comb it

Plait it—
    THERE!

Dorothy Mills

EGG THOUGHTS (soft-boiled)

I do not like the way you slide,
I do not like your soft inside,
I do not like you many ways,
And I could do for many days
Without a soft-boiled egg.

Russell Hoban

EGG TALK

I know a bloke
who, when he's got egg,
only eats yolk.
But it's all right
'cos his mate
eats the white.

Michael Rosen

HUMPTY DUMPTY

Humpty Dumpty
he got humpy
'cos his porridge was all lumpy
said, 'I'm not going to eat this muck
when I chew it – it all gets stuck.'

Michael Rosen

TOASTER TIME

Tick tick tick tick tick tick tick
Toast up a sandwich quick quick quick
Hamwich
Jamwich
Lick lick lick!

Tick tick tick tick tick tick – stop!
POP!

Eve Merriam

THE PICKETY FENCE

The pickety fence
The pickety fence
Give it a lick it's
The pickety fence
Give it a lick its
A clickety fence
Give it a lick its
A lickety fence
Give it a lick
Give it a lick
Give it a lick
With a rickety stick
Pickety
Pickety
Pickety
Pick

David McCord

JIGSAW PUDDLE

Sloshing my boot in the pavement puddle
I jiggle the sky above,

I fold the clouds in a sheep-like huddle,
I bobble the sun in the blue and white muddle—

And then I stand still—

Till the jigsaw puddle
Is smooth as a mirror again!

Emily Hearn

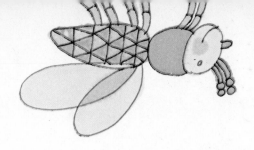

UPSIDE DOWN

It's funny how beetles
and creatures like that
can walk upside down
as well as walk flat.

They crawl on a ceiling
and climb on a wall
without any practice
or trouble at all.

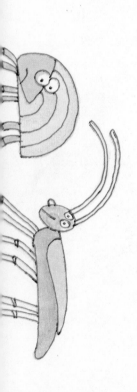

While I have been trying
for a year (maybe more)
and still I can't stand
with my head on the floor.

Aileen Fisher

WHISTLING

Oh, I can laugh and I can sing
and I can scream and shout,
but when I try to whistle,
the whistle won't come out.

I shape my lips the proper way,
I make them small and round,
but when I blow, just air comes out,
there is no whistling sound.

But I'll keep trying very hard
to whistle loud and clear,
and some day soon I'll whistle tunes
for everyone to hear.

Jack Prelutsky

DEBORAH DELORA

Deborah Delora, she liked a bit of fun –
She went to the baker's and bought a currant bun;
Dipped the bun in treacle and threw it at her teacher –
Deborah Delora! What a wicked creature!

Anon.

A LITTLE GIRL I HATE

I saw a little girl I hate
And kicked her with my toes.
She turned
And smiled
And KISSED me!
Then she punched me in the nose.

Arnold Spilka

THE MAN THAT HAD LITTLE TO SAY

I met a man at one o'clock who said

"Hello"   at two.

At three o'clock he looked at me and said,

"How do you do?"

At ten-to-four he said

"Good-bye"

and started on his way.

I'm glad he came to see me but he hadn't much to say.

John Ciardi

THE BALLOON

I went to the park
And I bought a balloon.
It sailed through the sky
Like a large orange moon.
It bumped and it fluttered
And swam with the clouds.
Small birds flew around it
In high chirping clouds.
It bounced and it balanced
And bowed with the breeze.
It skimmed past the leaves
On the tops of the trees.
And then as the day
Started turning to night
I gave a short jump
And I held the string tight
And home we all sailed
Through the darkening sky,
The orange balloon, the small birds
And I.

Karla Kuskin

FLASHLIGHT

My flashlight tugs me
through the dark
like a hound
with a yellow eye,

sniffs
at the edges
of steep places,

paws
at moles'
and rabbits'
holes,

points its nose
where sharp things
lie asleep–

and then it bounds
ahead of me
on home ground.

Judith Thurman

OUT IN THE DARK AND DAYLIGHT

Out in the dark and daylight,
under a cloud or tree,

Out in the park and play light,
out where the wind blows free,

Out in the March or May light
with shadows and stars to see,

Out in the dark and daylight . . .
that's where I like to be.

Aileen Fisher

AFTER A BATH

After my bath
I try, try, try
to wipe myself
till I'm dry, dry, dry.

Hands to wipe
and fingers and toes
and two wet legs
and a shiny nose.

Just think how much
less time I'd take
if I were a dog
and could shake, shake, shake.

Aileen Fisher

IF I WERE A FISH

Splash, splosh!
Whenever I wash
I wish and wish and wish
That I lived in the water all day long
Like a slithery, slippery fish.

Splash, splish!
If I were a fish
I wouldn't have to wash.
I wouldn't need soap or a towel or a sponge,
But I'd splish–
        And I'd splash–
                And I'd splosh!

Alison Winn

A BOOK IS A PLACE

A book is a place
where you can go
whenever you wish:
just open it up
and step in!

For if you can read

you can sail seven seas,

explore lost kingdoms
with magic keys . . .

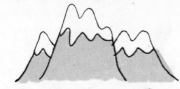

Climb snowy mountains,

Fly to the moon,

Speak with ghosts,

Hear mermaids croon . . .

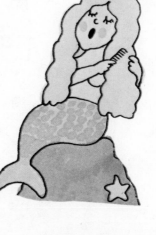

Swim with whales
through sea-green depths,

Tame wild horses and . . .

When you come back
& close your book
& sit there with a dreamy,
faraway look . . .

It's because you
know you can go
anywhere you want
whenever you wish—
just open a book
and step in!

Clyde Watson

BEDTIME STORIES

"Tell me a story,"

Says Witch's Child.

"About the Beast
So fierce and wild.

About a Ghost
That shrieks and groans.

A skeleton
That rattles bones.

About a Monster
Crawly-creepy.

Something nice
To make me sleepy."

Lilian Moore

NIGHT

up
   to bed   your head
   down on the pillow

up
   to chin   your covers
   warm and tight   tuck in
                         tuck in
                         tuck in

kiss
me
good

Arnold Adoff

ACKNOWLEDGEMENTS

Thanks are due to the following for permission to reprint copyright material: 'Days' reprinted by permission of Faber & Faber Ltd from *The Whitsun Weddings* by Philip Larkin; 'Waking' from Lilian Moore, *I Feel the Same Way*. Copyright © 1967 by Lilian Moore. Reprinted with the permission of Atheneum Publishers; David Higham Associates Limited for 'New Clothes and Old' by Eleanor Farjeon from *The Children's Bells* published by Oxford University Press, and 'Egg Thoughts' by Russell Hoban from *Egg Thoughts and Other Frances Songs* published by Faber & Faber; 'Hair' by Dorothy Mills from *Big Dipper*, edited by J. Epstein, J. Factor, G. Mackay and D. Rickards, published by Oxford University Press, Melbourne, Australia; Michael Rosen for 'Egg Talk' and 'Humpty Dumpty'. Copyright © Michael Rosen 1981; 'Toaster Time' from *There Is No Rhyme for Silver* by Eve Merriam. Copyright © 1962 by Eve Merriam. Reprinted by permission of the author.

'The Pickety Fence' from *One at a Time* by David McCord. Copyright © 1952 by David McCord. By permission of Little, Brown and Company, Boston, USA, and George G. Harrap & Company Limited, London; 'Jigsaw Puddle' by Emily Hearn. Used by permission of the author, first published in *Multipoems*, Nelson Canada Limited, 1972; Aileen Fisher for 'Upside Down' and 'After a Bath'; 'Whistling' from *Rainy Rainy Saturday* by Jack Prelutsky. Text copyright © 1980 by Jack Prelutsky. By permission of Greenwillow Books (A Division of William Morrow & Company); Frances Schwartz Literary Agency for 'A Little Girl I Hate' from *A Rumbudgin of Nonsense*. Copyright © 1970 by Arnold Spilka published by Charles Scribner's Sons. 'The Man That Had Little to Say' from *I Met a Man* by John Ciardi. Copyright © 1961 by John Ciardi. Reprinted by permission of Houghton Mifflin Company; Text of 'The Balloon' from *In the Middle of the Trees* by Karla Kuskin. Copyright © 1958 by Karla Kuskin. By permission of Harper & Row, Publishers, Inc.; 'Flashlight' from Judith Thurman, *Flashlight and Other Poems*. Copyright © 1976 by Judith Thurman. Reprinted by permission of Penguin Books Ltd and Atheneum Publishers, Inc.; Hodder & Stoughton Limited for 'If I Were a Fish' from *Swings and Things* by Alison Winn; 'A Book is a Place' by Clyde Watson reprinted by permission of Curtis Brown, Ltd, New York. Copyright © 1980 Clyde Watson; 1980 U.S. Children's Book Week poem, written for Children's Book Council, Inc.; 'Bedtime Stories' from Lilian Moore, *See My Lovely Poison Ivy*. Copyright © 1975 by Lilian Moore. Reprinted with permission of Atheneum Publishers; Text of 'Out in the Dark and Daylight' from *Out in the Dark and Daylight* by Aileen Fisher. Text copyright © 1980 by Aileen Fisher. By permission of Harper & Row, Publishers, Inc.; 'Night' from *Make a Circle to Keep Us In: Poems for a Good Day* by Arnold Adoff. Copyright © 1975 by Arnold Adoff. Reprinted by permission of Delacorte Press and Curtis Brown, Ltd, New York.

The Children's Choice® Clubhouse

It's the perfect place for playing or for curling up with a good book ★ Big enough to hold a few friends (it's 3' x 4½' and 4½' tall) ★ Made of sturdy corrugated cardboard with a washable finish ★ Decorated inside and out with whimsical illustrations in full color ★ A very special gift.

To order, please send your name and address with a check or money order for $19.95 to:

Children's Choice® Clubhouse
Scholastic Inc.
900 Sylvan Ave.
Englewood Cliffs
New Jersey 07632